ANTELOPE

A TRUE BOOK

by

Melissa Stewart

Children's Press®

A Division of Scholastic Inc.

New York Toronto London Auckland Sydney
Mexico City New Delhi Hong Kong
Danbury, Connecticut

A sable antelope

Reading Consultant
Nanci R. Vargus, Ed.D.
*Teacher in Residence
University of Indianapolis
Indianapolis, Indiana*

Content Consultant
Kathy Carlstead, Ph.D.
Honolulu Zoo

*Dedication:
To Colin Campbell Stewart*

*The photograph on the cover
shows an oryx.
The photograph on the
title page shows two
hartebeests.*

Library of Congress Cataloging-in-Publication Data

Stewart, Melissa.
    Antelope / Melissa Stewart.
        p. cm. — (A True book)
    Includes bibliographical references and index.
    Summary: Describes the physical characteristics of different kinds
of antelope, where they live, and their particular habits.
    ISBN 0-516-22198-1 (lib. bdg.)   0-516-26989-5 (pbk.)
    1. Antelope—Juvenile literature. [1. Antelope.] I. Title. II. Series.
    QL737.U53 S725 2002
    599.64'—dc21   2001047195

SCHOLASTIC and associated designs are trademarks and/or registered
trademarks of Scholastic Inc. CHILDREN'S PRESS, TRUE BOOKS, and A
TRUE BOOK and all associated designs are trademarks and/or registered
trademarks of Grolier Publishing Company, Inc.
1 2 3 4 5 6 7 8 9 10 R 11 10 09 08 07 06 05 04 03 02

Contents

Impala Are Antelope   5

All About Antelope   10

Antelope Are Mammals   18

Kinds of Antelope   26

Antelope in Our World   40

To Find Out More   44

Important Words   46

Index   47

Meet the Author   48

Two impala
grazing on an
African plain

Impala Are Antelope

As the sun begins to set and the African air slowly cools, a small herd of impala grazes on the dry, grassy plains. The animals take quick bites and swallow the grass right down. There will be plenty of time to grind the plants up later.

Why are these antelope eating in such a hurry? They never know when a hungry lion or cheetah might show up. They must always stay alert and be ready to flee.

For impala, there is safety in numbers. It is harder for a predator to sneak up on a group because each animal is always on the lookout for signs of danger. If one animal hears a sound or detects the scent of an enemy, it warns

A herd of impala

the others and the whole group
bounds away at lightning speed.
The impala is one of the
fastest animals in the world. It
can run at a speed of 45 miles

The impala is one of the world's fastest land animals.

(72 kilometers) per hour
and leap more than 30 feet
(9 meters) at a time.

Impala are just one of the
nearly 100 kinds of antelope
in the world. Some kinds of
antelope live in Asia, but most

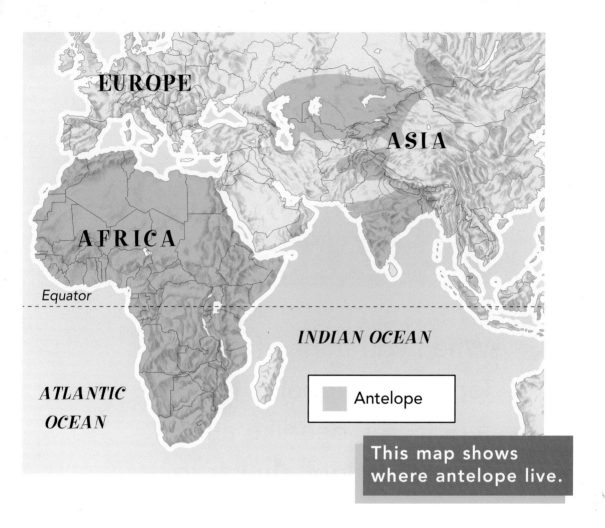

The map shows where antelope live.

live in eastern and southern Africa. Some antelope live in swamps, deserts, and forests, but most live on open grasslands.

All About Antelope

When you think of an antelope, you probably picture a graceful, deerlike animal. Impala do look similar to deer, but many other antelope do not. The royal antelope is as small as a rabbit, while the eland is as big as an ox.

The suni (above), only 12 to 16 inches (31 to 41 cm) tall, is one of the smallest antelope. The eland (left) is the largest antelope.

All male antelope and most female antelope have horns. Each kind of antelope has unique horns. For example, impala have upward-curving horns, but oryx have long, straight horns. Elands have

Duikers (top left), impala (above), and oryx (bottom left) all have different-shaped horns.

spiraled horns, while duikers have short, spiky horns.

A deer sheds its antlers every year, but an antelope keeps the same set of horns for its entire life. An antelope's horns are hollow and fit over a bony core that grows out of the animal's skull.

Antelope are closely related to cattle, sheep, and goats. All these animals have large, flat teeth, and feet with a split hoof that protects their two toes.

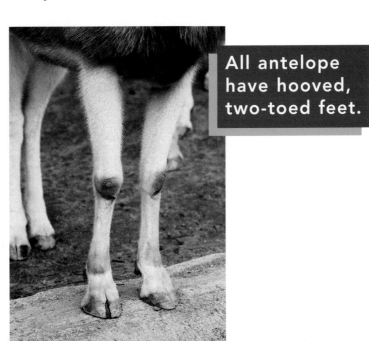

All antelope have hooved, two-toed feet.

Although these animals sometimes eat leaves, twigs, bark, buds, and fruit, their main source of food is grass.

Grass is hard to digest, so antelope and their relatives do something unusual. When the animals are resting, they regurgitate—they force food from their stomach back up into their mouth. Then they chew it long and hard. This is called "chewing cud."

A bongo chewing its cud

Most antelope live in dry places and can survive without drinking much water. They rarely stop for a drink at a water hole. Most of their water comes from the plants they eat.

Food For All

A wildebeest

A sweeping look across an African plain may provide views of small groups of impala, gazelles, wildebeest, topi, and other antelope. Often, several kinds of antelope graze close to

Thomson's gazelles

A dik-dik

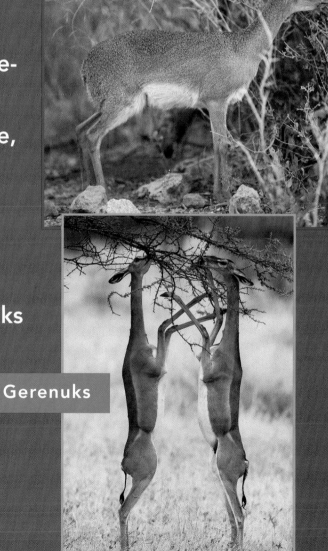

one another. This is possible because antelope do not compete for food. For example, wildebeest eat tall grasses, while impala and gazelle prefer shorter grasses. In forested areas, dik-diks munch on low leaves and twigs, while gerenuks stretch to reach branches high above their heads.

Gerenuks

Antelope Are Mammals

Antelope, cattle, sheep, and goats belong to a large group of animals called mammals. Dogs, elephants, guinea pigs, and humans are mammals too. All mammals have a backbone that supports their body and helps them move.

18

Like all antelope, this female waterbuck and calf are mammals.

They also have lungs and breathe air. They are warm-blooded animals, so their body temperature stays about the same no matter how cold or warm it is around them.

A bongo (right) and
a bushbuck (below)

Most mammals have hairy bodies and four legs. Many antelope are covered with a smooth coat of brown or gray hair. Some antelope have coats of just one color. Other antelope, such as bongos, reedbuck, bushbuck, and kudu, have markings that help the animals blend in with their surroundings.

All baby mammals grow inside their mother until they are ready to be born. When it is time to give birth, the mother

A Thomson's gazelle
licking her newborn calf

antelope leaves her herd and
goes to a safe place. She usually has one baby at a time.

Like all baby mammals, a
young antelope drinks its
mother's milk. The calves of

small and medium-sized antelope stay hidden until they are
ready to start eating plants.
Their mothers visit the babies
several times a day to feed
them. The rest of the time
mothers guard their young from
a safe distance.

After a few weeks, the calves
are ready to travel with the
herd. But they will continue to
drink some mother's milk until
they are about 4 months old.

The calves of large antelope,
such as oryx and addax, are too

A nyala calf nurses while its mother takes a long drink of water.

big to hide from their enemies. They quickly must learn to walk, and they follow their mothers around all day long. Like their smaller cousins, they start to graze after a few weeks. But they may continue to nurse for up to 9 months.

Wildebeest calves must quickly learn to keep up with the herd.

Kinds of Antelope

Many scientists divide antelope into seven groups depending on their size, where they live, and their habits.

The duikers are a group of small and medium-sized antelope that live in forests. They feed at night on leaves, twigs, and fallen fruit.

These antelope have a wide
mouth, small ears, a rounded
back, short legs, and short
straight horns. Duikers live alone
or in very small groups. Each

Dwarf antelope include the klipspringer (bottom left), steenbok (top), and oribi (bottom right).

male has a territory that he will defend against other males.

Dwarf antelope are very small animals with large ears, a narrow muzzle, short spiky horns, and a short tail. This group includes the royal antelope—the smallest antelope—as well as the suni, the dik-dik, the steenbok, the klipspringer, and the oribi.

Like duikers, dwarf antelope usually live alone or in small groups. When these nervous little animals sense danger, they lie down and stay perfectly still. If an enemy gets too close, dwarf antelope jump into the air and dart to safety.

The gazelles are a very large group of graceful, medium-sized antelope. In addition to nine kinds of gazelles, the group includes springboks, dibatags, gerenuks, and impala. These animals usually live in large herds on open grasslands. The most unusual

Springboks live in large herds.

member of this group is the
gerenuk. If it sees some tasty
leaves or branches above its
head, it stands on its back legs
to reach the food.

Lechwes like to live close to water.

You can probably guess why water-loving antelope are grouped together. They all like to live close to water. These antelope have long necks and bodies, but would rather hide than run from enemies. Waterbucks, pukus, reedbucks, lechwes, and kob antelope may live in herds or on their own. Males have thin, ridged, gently curving horns, but females have no horns at all.

The addax, oryx, roan antelope, and sable antelope belong to a group known as the horse antelope. These animals are large and strong with muscular legs, striped faces, long ridged horns, a short mane, and a long tail. They usually run from predators, but sometimes they put up a fight. They can defend themselves by kicking an attacker with their powerful legs or jabbing it with their horns.

An addax (above) and a roan antelope (left)

Bonteboks (left) and hartebeest (below) are large antelope that can run fast and far.

Hartebeest, wildebeest, bonteboks, hirolas, and topi are part of a separate group of large antelope. These animals have high shoulders, long thin legs, and long bushy tails. Their bodies are built for running fast and far. They often form herds made up of one male and several females and their young. Sometimes many herds join together and migrate long distances in search of food and water.

A nyala buck (right) and nilgai calves (below)

The last group of antelope are lumped together because they all have spiraling horns. The eland, bongo, bushbuck, kudu, nyala, nilgai, chousingha, and sitatunga would all rather hide from predators than flee. When they are in a group, their markings make it hard to tell where one animal starts and another ends.

Antelope in Our World

Antelope have more than a dozen natural predators. Some of the most dangerous are lions, cheetahs, leopards, hyenas, jackals, and wild dogs. Human hunters kill antelope too. For hundreds of years, native peoples have hunted antelope for their meat and

A cheetah chasing a Thomson's gazelle

hides. More recently, hunters from other parts of the world have killed thousands of antelope for sport.

Blueboks died out about 200 years ago.

As a result of all this hunting, the bluebok has vanished from Earth forever. Many other kinds of antelope are also in danger of disappearing. Even antelope that are still common may soon face trouble if people continue to destroy the land they live on. We must do everything we can to protect these beautiful animals.

If we do not protect antelope like this kudu buck, they may disappear from Earth.

To Find Out More

Here are some additional resources to help you learn more about antelope:

Books

Halliburton, Warren J. **African Wildlife.** Crestwood, 1992.

Hoffman, Mary. **Antelope: Animals in the Wild.** Raintree/Steck-Vaughn, 1990.

Patent, Dorothy Hinshaw. **Why Mammals Have Fur.** Cobblehill Books, 1995.

Stewart, Melissa. **Mammals.** Children's Press, 2001.

Organizations and Online Sites

International Wildlife Coalition

70 East Falmouth Highway
East Falmouth, MA, USA
02536
http://www.iwc.org

The IWC works to save endangered species and preserve animal habitats and the environment.

KidsGoWild

*http://wcs.org/sites/
kidsgowild*

This is the kids' page of the Wildlife Conservation Society. It includes wildlife news, wild animal facts, and information on how kids can get involved in saving wild animals and the environment by joining Conservation Kids.

The Ultimate Ungulate

*http://www.ultimateu
ngulate.com/*

If you click your mouse on "Artiodactyla" (even-toed ungulates) and then "Bovidae" (the animal group that includes antelope, cows, and sheep), you will call up links to Web pages that describe a variety of antelope, including impala, hartebeest, blesboks, hirolas, and many others.

Important Words

buck name for the males of some kinds of mammals, including antelope

calf name for the young of some kinds of mammals, including antelope

mammal warm-blooded animal that has a backbone and fur and feeds its young mother's milk

migrate to travel long distances in search of food, water, or a place to mate

predator animal that hunts and kills other animals for food

regurgitate to bring food from the stomach back up into the mouth so that it can be thoroughly chewed

shed to come off

unique one of a kind

Index

(**Boldface** page numbers indicate illustrations.)

addax, 23, 34, **35**
Africa, 9
Asia, 8
bluebok, 42, **42**
bongo, **15, 20,** 21, 39
bontebok, **36,** 37
bushbuck, **20,** 21, 39
calves, **24, 19,** 22, **22,** 23, **38**
chewing cud, 14
chousingha, 39
dibatag, 30
dik-dik, 17, **17,** 29
duiker, 12, 26, 27, **27**
dwarf antelope, **28,** 29, 30
ears, 27, 29
eland, 10, 11, **11, 12,** 39
food, 14, 16, 17, **16-17**
gazelles, 16, 17, 30
gerenuk, 17, **17,** 30, 31
habitats of antelope, 5, 9, 16, 30
hartebeest, **2, 36,** 37
herds, 30, 37
hirola, 37
horns, 11, 12, 13, 27, 29, 33, 34
horse antelope, 34

hunting of antelope, 40, 41, 42
impala, **4,** 5, 6, 7, **7,** 8, **8,** 10, 11, **12,** 16, 17, 30
klipspringer, **28,** 29
kob antelope, 33
kudu, 21, 39, **43**
lechwe, **32,** 33
map of where antelope live, **9**
markings, 39
migration, 37
nilgai, **38,** 39
nyala, **24, 38,** 39
oribi, **28,** 29
oryx, **cover,** 11, **12,** 23, 34
predators, 6, 24, 30, 39, 40
puku, 33
reedbuck, 21, 33
roan antelope, 34, **35**
royal antelope, 10, 29
sable antelope, 34
sitatunga, 39
springbok, 30, **31**
steenbok, **28,** 29
suni, **11,** 29
Thomson's gazelles, **17, 22, 41**
topi, 16, 37
waterbuck, **19,** 33
wildebeest, 16, **16,** 17, **25,** 37

Meet the Author

A few years ago, Melissa Stewart visited the African countries of Kenya and Tanzania. While on safari, she saw a wide variety of antelope, including impala, gazelle, topi, oryx, wildebeest, reedbucks, dik-diks, and eland. Her favorite antelope is the gerenuk.

Ms. Stewart earned a bachelor's degree in biology from Union College and a master's degree in science and environmental journalism from New York University. The inspiration for many of the children's books she has written comes from her travels, but she also enjoys spending time observing the wildlife near her home in Marlborough, Massachusetts.